EDUCATION AND THE FOUNDATIONS OF HUMAN FREEDOM

HORACE MANN LECTURE, 1962

EDUCATION AND THE FOUNDATIONS OF HUMAN FREEDOM

BY

GEORGE S. COUNTS

Visiting Distinguished Professor of Education
Southern Illinois University

PITTSBURGH
UNIVERSITY OF PITTSBURGH PRESS
1962

LIBRARY OF CONGRESS CATALOG
CARD NO. 62-

HORACE MANN LECTURES

THE HORACE MANN
LECTURESHIP

To commemorate the life of Horace Mann, 1796-1859, and in recognition of his matchless services to the American Public School System, the School of Education of the University of Pittsburgh, in cooperation with the Tri-State Area School Study Council, established the Horace Mann Lectureship. The striking and varied Contributions of Horace Mann must ever be kept alive and be re-emphasized in each generation. It is difficult, indeed, to assess the magnitude of Mann's educational services. Turning from the profession of law he devoted his life to the study and improvement of education. He, more than any other, can truly be called "Father of the American Public School System." His boundless energy, coupled with a brilliant and penetrating mind, focused the attention of the citizens of his era on the need for the improvement and sup-

PORT OF PUBLIC SCHOOLS. HIS SERVICES WERE MANIFOLD. IT SHALL BE THE PURPOSE OF THESE LECTURES TO RE-AFFIRM HIS FAITH IN FREE SCHOOLS AND TO CALL TO THEIR SERVICE ALL CITIZENS OF THIS GENERATION. IT IS VITAL THAT ALL UNDERSTAND THE PURPOSE AND FUNCTION OF A FREE PUBLIC SCHOOL SYSTEM IN AMERICAN DEMOCRACY.

THE HORACE MANN LECTURES ARE PUBLISHED ANNUALLY BY THE UNIVERSITY OF PITTSBURGH PRESS.

EDUCATION AND THE
FOUNDATIONS
OF HUMAN FREEDOM

THE LAND OF LIBERTY

NINE SCORE and six years ago "our fathers brought forth on this continent a new nation conceived in liberty and dedicated to the proposition that all men are created equal." And now, as in Lincoln's day, we are engaged in a great struggle, "testing whether that nation or any nation so conceived and so dedicated can long endure." The reference of these words of the Great Emancipator, as we all know, is to the Declaration of Independence, perhaps the most eloquent expression in the history of man of the age-old faith in human freedom.

In the period that witnessed the founding and launching of the Republic we experienced a sense of destiny. Inspired by the ideas of the Enlightenment, we were convinced that we were blazing a bold new trail into the future, a trail that other peoples would follow. In his first inaugural Washington gave expression to this conviction in words that must never die. "The preservation of the sacred fire of liberty and the destiny of the republican model of government," he said, "are justly considered as *deeply*, perhaps as *finally*, staked on the experiment intrusted to the hands of the American people." A generation later Daniel Webster, in his Bunker Hill Oration, repeated the challenge of our first president: "If, in our case, the representative system ultimately fail, popular governments must be pronounced impossible. No combination of circumstances more favorable to the experiment can ever be expected to occur. The last hopes of mankind, therefore, rest with us; and if it should be proclaimed that our example had become an argument against the experiment, the knell of popular liberty would be sounded throughout the world."

We were indeed a fortunate and favored people. We were the beneficiaries of an unprecedented "combination of circumstances." First of all, we were the legatees of the long struggle of the Eng-

lish people for freedom, from the Magna
Carta of 1215 to the Bill of Rights of
1689, and after. We were the possessors
of a fabulous land, vast, rich, beautiful,
and protected by the great oceans. Power
in both its military and its economic
forms was relatively widely distributed.
Significantly, Alexis de Tocqueville begins his brilliant treatise on American
democracy in 1835 with a reference, not
to our political ideas and practices, but
to the "general equality of condition
among the people." Ralph Waldo Emer-
son stressed the absence of feudal institutions and traditions. "America," he
wrote, "was opened after the feudal mis-
chief was spent, and so the people made
a good start. We began well. No inquisi-
tion here, no kings, no nobles, no dom-
inant church. Here heresy has lost its
terrors."

The passing of the years confirmed
our faith in this promise of America. To
be sure, from the day of its birth our
social and political system aroused the
ridicule and hostility of the privileged
orders of the Old World. But we general-

ly regarded these adversaries as survivals from the past and destined to be
swept aside by the spread of enlightenment and the irresistible march toward
the emancipation of the human race.
America became the "haven of refuge"
for the oppressed and the "land of the
free" for all who could reach her shores.
We were certain that history itself was
working on our side and that our political ideas would triumph everywhere. For
generations this view was widely shared
by exploited classes and idealistic elements beyond the oceans. Said Gladstone,
"the American Constitution is . . . the
most wonderful work ever struck off at
a given time by the brain and purpose of
man." And that our achievement in the
realm of popular rule, with all of its im-
perfections, has been phenomenal cannot be denied. Indeed, the maintenance
for almost two centuries of a constitutional system on the foundations of popular freedom must be ranked among the
miracles in the long history of political
institutions. Shortly before his death,
Charles A. Beard, one of our foremost

students of the founding of the Republic, in response to a query by a distinguished Chinese scholar and diplomat regarding America's contribution to the advancement of civilization, put in first place: "The establishment of a regime of liberty over a vast region." Unquestionably, in the realm of the spirit — here is our greatest achievement. If we falter here, our history will have lost its meaning, and the forebodings of Washington, Jefferson, Webster, and Lincoln will have been fulfilled.

Our early sense of destiny was given expression in the Great Seal of the United States which proclaims *Novus Ordo Seclorum*, New Order of the Ages, and which is stamped on the dollar bill. One wonders whether the ordinary American citizen ever sees these Latin words or knows what they mean. It seems probable that he sees only the dollar sign and accepts that sign as the symbol of the Republic. This raises the big question regarding the subject of the Horace Mann Lecture of the year: Have we lost our sense of dedication to the "cause of liberty?" Although presidential commissions and private associations and individuals have been inquiring into the condition of our liberties and the goals of our society, we seem to be chiefly concerned with defending something vaguely called the "American Way of Life" rather than with fulfilling the "promise of America." In other words, we appear to think that in the sphere of moral values we have arrived and that there is nothing more to do but to increase our material conforts.

Leo Perla in his perceptive book, *Can We End the Cold War?,* issues the following challenge: "The values by which our world has lived and is now about to die, unless something is done swiftly, will have to be rearranged. At present their order of importance is: (1) money, (2) power, (3) material possessions, (4) cleanliness, (5) intelligence and education, and (6) moral qualities. Our survival depends upon how swiftly and successfully we place 'moral qualities' first and 'money' last." This statement probably does less than justice to our scale of values. The fact must be recognized that ours, like every free society, is a pluralistic society and that there are vast differences among us. Yet, but four years ago one Sunday evening in September, just before the schools were to open, I heard two different voices on two different radio stations urging the youth to complete their high school education. The one and only reason given was that it would be worth "fifty-thousand dollars." Clearly this admonition did not come from any annual report of Horace Mann, "the father of the common school." It does seem that the major motivating force which inspires the young to enter the higher schools of the land is the promise of material success.

We repeat the words of the Declaration of Independence, the Federal Constitution, the Bill of Rights, the Gettysburg Address, and the "Four Freedoms." But our actions often fail to honor our professions. This condition led Gunnar Myrdal, the distinguished Swedish social scientist, to choose as a title for his monumental study of race relations in the United States, *An American Dilemma*. At the beginning of his first chapter he states "America, compared to every other country in Western civilization, large or small, has the *most explicitly expressed* system of general ideals in reference to human interrelations," and "this body of ideals is more widely understood and appreciated than similar ideals are anywhere else." This body of ideals he calls the American Creed. It is a priceless possession, but, if it is to survive, it must be made increasingly explicit in our way of life. Here lies the "dilemma."

Today our unique place in history is being challenged to its very foundations. That great "reservoir of good will" toward America which Wendell Wilkie sensed in his world journey two decades ago has been seriously depleted. In terms of the cause of human freedom, if the advance of totalitarianism is not halted, "we will have to face," in the words of Bronislaw Malinowski, the great Polish anthropologist, "a period of dark ages, indeed the darkest ages of human history." And in his inaugural address in January, 1961, President Kennedy challenged us to be worthy of our tradition of liberty and the vision of the founders of the Republic. "In the long history of the world," he said, "only a few generations have been granted the role of defending freedom in its hour of maximum danger." In my opinion this is precisely the role which history has assigned to our people in these days. Thus, the challenge of our first president has come full circle. We have entered the most fateful period in the history of our country, not excepting the period of the struggle between the states. Some voices are heard in the land to the effect that it is "better to be Red than Dead." These, of course, are not the voices of liberty. Rather, they are the voices of the frightened. But let us take a brief and candid look at the world of the twentieth century and the place of America therein. We may then consider in perspective the role of education in the cause of human freedom today.

The Challenge of These Times

We have come to the end of an epoch
in the brief history of our country and
in the long history of mankind. In the
second edition (1962) of *The Story of
Man,* which traces the human record
"from the first human to primitive culture and beyond," its author, the noted
anthropologist, Carleton S. Coon, states
that man, having passed through three
phases of history, now stands "on the
threshold of phase four." And he suggests at the close of his account that "the
alternative to cultural change is not a
perpetuation of the status quo, but the
failure of a cosmic experiment, the end
of man's great adventures." This observation brings to mind the work of a German historian, Egon Friedell. In the late
twenties he published *A Cultural History
of the Modern Age.* The account begins
with the Black Death in the fourteenth
century and ends with the start of the
First World War. He explains his closing of the account in 1914 by saying that
the Modern Age ended in that year, that

a new age opened, and that he did not understand it. His subsequent career provides a fitting climax to the story. After Hitler came to power Friedell went to live in Vienna. Then one day in 1938, following the seizure of Austria by the Nazis, as he was sitting in his upper-story apartment, he heard a knock on the door. On opening the door, he saw two members of the Gestapo, the Nazi political police. Sensing their mission, he turned immediately, ran to the window, opened it, and jumped to his death. Obviously, as Norman Cousins observed years later, "modern man is obsolete."

In his monumental study of the twenty-one civilizations which the races of man have created on the earth, of which only five survive, Arnold J. Toynbee observes that every civilization or society sooner or later experiences a "time of troubles" occasioned by powerful new forces arising either from within or from without. We are living today in such a "time of troubles." But this one is to be distinguished from its many predecessors in the long history of mankind, which have sometimes marked the end of great civilizations and the destruction of "eternal" cities, by the fact that all mankind, and not just one people or continent, is ineluctably involved. It is an age of revolution as wide as the planet. The very structure of the world is being profoundly altered. Already we have witnessed, almost without number, political, social, economic, military, scientific, technological, moral, and even religious revolutions. It is an age which, in the words of Bertrand Russell, promises that "the near future must be either much better or much worse than the past." It is an age in which the impossible follows swiftly on the heels of the impossible.

In the early autumn of 1938, following the signing of the Munich Pact, which, according to one of its authors, was "to bring peace in our time," but which actually cleared the way for Hitler to launch his mad crusade to destroy the best in Western civilization, Anne O'Hare MacCormick, one of our best informed and most perceptive commentators on foreign affairs, wrote in her column in *The New York Times* that "all of those things are happening in the world that could not happen." These words constitute one of the most penetrating and disturbing characterizations of the world in which we live and should be inscribed over the door of every school in the land. Mrs. MacCormick knew, of course, that things don't happen that can't happen. She was merely employing a literary figure to dramatize the obvious fact that so many things are happening that could not happen if our premises about the world were sound. In a word, we continue, in the tradition of the human race, to think from premises derived from a world that has passed or is passing away. In the same column, Mrs. MacCormick reported the case of a European newspaper editor who had resigned his post, not because of outstide pressure, but because he no longer understood his world and consequently did not know what to say about it.

In order to view our times in perspective let us turn to a volume published in 1913 by one of the most distinguished

English students of the history of political ideas, James B. Bury. In this work, published one year before the catastrophe of the First World War struck the Western World and entitled *A History of Freedom of Thought,* the author gives an account of the struggle from ancient times to establish the precious right of man to think and thus do honor to that quality of *homo sapiens* which distinguishes it from all other living things. In the final chapter he thus formulates his conclusion: "The struggle of reason against authority has ended in what appears to be a decisive and permanent victory for liberty. In the most civilized and progressive countries, freedom of discussion is recognized as a fundamental principle." Here is a relic from what would seem to be a distant past rather than a generalization appearing in this twentieth century of the Christian era.

To be fair to Bury, however, something should be added. Being a good historian, he knew that prediction is hazardous. Consequently, after registering the optimism expressed above, he began to wonder. Glancing at the past and re-calling the recurrent ages of darkness, he wrote: "Is it not conceivable that something of the same kind may occur again? That some new force, emerging from the unknown, may surprise the world and cause a similar set-back." With this query he turned to the present of 1913 and engaged in the following extraordinary and prophetic speculation: "It is by no means inconceivable that in lands where opinion is now free coercion might be introduced. If a revolutionary social movement prevailed, led by men inspired by faith in formulas (like the men of the French Revolution) and resolved to impose their creed, experience shows that coercion would almost inevitably be resorted to." And this is precisely what happened in many parts of the world. During the succeeding generation, probably more men, women, youth and even children were sent to the crematorium, the execution chamber, or something approaching slavery for political dissent, religious belief, or ethnic origin than during any like period in history.

And the age of hatred and violence continues in the second half of the twentieth century.

With Bury's volume as a bench-mark let us pass in brief review a few of the impossible things that have happened in our world since 1913, beginning with the First World War. When this fateful struggle began in August, 1914, and the "lights went out" in Europe, we in America were aghast. We had been confident that the statesmen of the Old World would never permit their differences to reach the stage of an internecine conflict which might wreck Western civilization. And after it started, we were certain that either the wisdom of the leaders or the tremendous cost of the conflict in men and resources would bring an early settlement. At any rate, in spite of our sympathies with one side or the other, we firmly resolved that we would not be drawn into the holocaust. We remembered well the counsel of Washington about becoming involved in "entangling alliances." But when we finally entered the struggle on the side of the "democracies," the Russian revolution having occurred, we did so under the slogan of "A War to Make the World Safe for Democracy." And when victory was won, we were certain that this end had been achieved. For had not the three great autocracies of central and eastern Europe, survivals from the "age of kings," been overthrown by popular revolts? It was clear to all "right-thinking" people that democracy had triumphed everywhere and was certain to continue its triumphant march throughout the world. Few indeed imagined that on the ruins of the House of the Romanovs and the House of the Hohenzollerns there would rise new despotisms vastly more tyrannical than the political systems they displaced.

Thus, the birth of totalitarianism was something that just could not happen in the enlightened twentieth century. When Lenin with his tiny Party of Bolsheviks seized power by armed force on November 7, 1917, and established his dictatorship in the name of the proletariat, we knew that his regime could not endure, because he proceeded to violate the laws of classical economics, which, of course, had the authority of the laws of nature. And no one can violate the laws of nature and prosper. In Italy Mussolini formed his party of Black Shirts to combat Bolshevism, marched on Rome in October, 1922, overthrew the parliamentary system, announced the end of liberalism, and proclaimed as his goal the revival of the glories of the Ancient Roman Empire. Then in Germany, an obscure corporal of Austrian birth first attracted the attention of the world by his ridiculous and futile "beer-hall putsch" in Munich in November, 1923. Arrested and sent to prison, he wrote his *Mein Kampf* in which he candidly outlined his ideas, policies, intentions, and methods. Nobody took him seriously because it was obvious to any "sound thinker" that this little man with the Charlie Chaplin moustache and his barbarous doctrines of anti-Semitism and Nordic supremacy could never hope to triumph in the most literate of the great nations, of which he was not even a citizen. As one reads

William L. Shirer's *The Rise and Fall of the Third Reich,* the entire story passes understanding. These things simply could not have happened, even though we know they did. It is illuminating to note that an American college student before the First World War never read or heard four words which were destined to play such a tremendous role during the succeeding generation. These four words are Bolshevism, Fascism, Nazism, and totalitarianism. In fact, these words could not be found in the dictionaries until years after the establishment of the regimes which they represented. The word "totalitarianism" appeared for the first time in Webster's Unabridged International Dictionary in 1934!

In the autumn of 1929 came the "great depression." Although we had experienced depressions more or less periodically since 1762, in scope, depth, and duration this one surpassed all of its predecessors. The entire economy was paralyzed, banks closed their doors, the total national income was reduced by more than one-half, and between thirteen and fifteen million men and women joined the ranks of the unemployed. For the first time in our history, America, the fabled land of youth, was confronted with a "youth problem." Thousands of young people wandered over the country looking for something to do, and eventually we established the National Youth Administration and launched the Civilian Conservation Corps. For several years following the crash on the stock market, many of our foremost industrial and political leaders assured our people that the economy was fundamentally sound and that "prosperity was just around the corner." With the coming of the new administration in 1933, heroic measures were adopted to put the economy back on its feet, but without too much success. In fact, it was not until the start of the Second World War that full employment returned. During this period millions of Americans began to lose faith in their institutions, the doctrines of Communism appealed to many, and the banners of the "crooked cross" were raised in the "land of the free." The experience of these years, both at home and abroad, shows that men do not love political liberty above all else; and that, if they are forced to choose between jobs and liberty, many will choose jobs, or even the promise of jobs. The "great depression" was something that could not happen to the American people.

The list of things happening that could not happen should also include the reforms of the New Deal, the Second World War, the disaster at Pearl Harbor, the creation of the atomic bomb, the formation of the United Nations with headquarters in New York City, the triumph of Communism in China, the launching of the first *sputnik* by a despotic "backward country," the orbiting of the earth in ninety minutes, the dissolution of the colonial empires, the emergence on the world stage of Sukarno, Adoula, Tshombe, and Touré, the establishment of a Communist regime on the island of Cuba, the allocation of billions for the exploration of the universe, and the sober contemplation of the probable existence of intelligent creatures on

other planets. And the list might be further extended. We have been, we are,
and we shall be living in a very strange
world indeed. In fact, we find ourselves
living in a Utopia according to the original meaning of the word—Nowhere.

If we turn our minds back to the closing years of the nineteenth century and
the beginning of the twentieth, we find
little prevision of what was destined to
happen. In 1879, Victor Hugo, address-
ing a Workingmen's Congress in Mar-
seilles, presented the following picture
of the future of mankind: "In the twentieth century war will be dead, the scaf-
fold will be dead, hatred will be dead,
royalty will be dead, frontier boundaries
will be dead, dogmas will be dead; man
will live. He will possess something higher than all these—a great country, the
whole earth, and a great hope, the whole
heaven. . . . Let us salute it, this beautiful
twentieth century which will possess our
children, which our children will possess." William C. Bullitt, a distinguished
diplomat, looking backward from 1946,
pointed to "the early morning atmos-

phere in which men lived in that age which is separated from today by so few years but by such mountainous and disastrous events." After noting the abolition of slavery and the general advance of free institutions, he observed: "Mutual trust was so great among civilized nations that passports were not required anywhere in the world except in four backward countries: Russia, Turkey, Bulgaria, and Japan. Barriers to international trade were low, and currency restrictions did not exist. Five European nations, France, Belgium, Switzerland, Italy and Greece, indeed, had made their coined monies interchangeable." Max Beloff, Oxford historian, stated in 1951 that, before Sarajevo "nowhere in Europe was it possible to take the same gloomy view of the future that the present generation has come to regard as almost normal" and that "the characteristic of the last period of old Europe was something which can best be described as the rule of law." The developments in the field of technology also were not foreseen. In 1885, Carrol D. Wright,

United States Commissioner of Labor
and a distinguished citizen, made the following prognostication: "It is true that
new processes of manufacture will un-
doubtedly continue, and this will be an
ameliorating influence, but it will not
leave room for a marked extension, such
as has been witnessed during the last
fifty years." There were, of course, dis-
senters from this generally optimistic
and complacent view of the future.
Shortly before he died in 1910, William
Graham Sumner, our foremost sociolo-
gist, made a striking observation and
prophecy: "I have lived through the best
period of my country's history. The next
generations are going to see war and
social calamities. I am glad I don't have
to live on into them." Four years after
his death, the first of the great catas-
trophes of "this beautiful twentieth century" hit the Western world. And, of
course, Karl Marx and his followers pre-
dicted the end of "capitalism" and a
world proletarian revolution.

Underlying this "time of troubles"
and disrupting the ancient ways of man

is a new force which entered Western culture with power but a few centuries ago and which in the present century is advancing with incredible and ever accelerating speed. The new force is called science and, when applied to the ways of life, technology. "Of all the elements of modern culture," wrote Preserved Smith a generation ago in his *A History of Modern Culture,* "as of all the forces moulding modern life, science has been the greatest. It can be shown that all other changes in society are largely dependent on this. Thought, philosophy, religion, art, education, laws, morals, economic institutions, are to a great extent dependent on the progress of science. Not only does science alter the technique in the production of wealth, but it alters man's view of the world in which he lives." And we in America in particular have come to identify "progress," to which we are thoroughly committed, with the advancement of science, and especially technology. Progress means more gadgets, more labor-saving devices, more speed in transportation and communication, more material comforts. Indeed, a page entitled "Parade of Progress," which appears weekly in a number of our newspapers, confines itself to these things.

It is at this point that we have lost our way. We seem not to realize that human culture has an organic quality, that its various elements are functionally interrelated, and that it develops severe strains and tensions when some powerful element changes much more rapidly than the others. Our troubles today arise largely from the fact that, as yet, we have by no means learned how to live with this new force, how to discipline its energies and make the necessary adjustments in our institutions, our outlook on the world, and our system of values. We should be pondering the wise words of Stanley Casson, a distinguished English archaeologist, who, in 1937, published a book in which he traced the theme of "progress and catastrophe" as far back as the human record would take him. He concludes his study with this warning: "When his practical inventiveness ran ahead of his moral consciousness and social organization, then man has equally faced destruction. Perhaps today we are in this stage." And these words were probably written a full decade before the first atomic bomb exploded over the deserts of New Mexico on July 16, 1945. Certainly, our "practical inventiveness" has rendered obsolete both our *operating* "moral consciousness" and our "social organization." Fortunately, some of our most brilliant scientists are aware of this fateful lag in our culture. Detlew W. Bronk thus advised a House Committee in 1947: "I cannot think of any field of research in physical science which does not ultimately lead, and usually very promptly, to new social problems. The same is true in biology and medicine. It is important, therefore, that competent social scientists should work hand in hand with the natural scientists, so that problems may be solved as they arise, and so that many of them may not arise in the first instance." Wernher Von Braun, foremost authority on rockets, warns: "If the world's ethical standards

fail to rise with the advance of our technological revolution, we shall all perish."
And long before the dawn of the atomic age Henry Adams made the following remarkable observation: "Man has mounted science and is now run away with. I firmly believe that, before many centuries more, science will be master of man. The engines he will have invented will be beyond his strength to control. Some day science will have the existence of man in its power, and the human race will commit suicide by blowing up the world."

The momentum of the advance of this powerful element in human culture should receive the most sober and sustained attention. We must beware of the mentality of the head of the United States Patent Office who, in 1833, offered "to resign because he felt that the limit of human invention had been reached and there would be no further need for his services." We must realize that, if the human race survives, we are still in the early stages of scientific discovery and invention. We can no longer afford the luxury of comforting ourselves with the thought that at last all the great and revolutionary advances in this realm have been made. The exact reverse is probably much closer to the truth. In his *Man the Maker,* a history of engineering published in 1950 after the dawn of the atomic age, R. J. Forbes of the University of Amsterdam warns us that "we have picked up but a few pebbles on the shores of a vast ocean which remains to be explored." May it not be that the overarching task of our total program of education is to close this gap between our "practical inventiveness" and our "moral consciousness and social organization"— and to close it in the shortest possible period of time? Otherwise the gap will grow wider with every passing year. But to this question we have given little thought. The level of our understanding of the nature of this "time of troubles" is revealed in the National Defense Education Act recently enacted by the Congress of the United States. That act seems to be based on the presupposition that science and mathematics will save us, whereas the very most that these

things can do in the present struggle for
the world is to give us time to save ourselves. The great challenge to education
is in the realm of understanding and
values. What we really need are statesmen, philosophers, and prophets of the
stature of the founding fathers of the
Republic, and a free people capable of
recognizing and honoring them.

SOME OF THE REALITIES OF THE AGE

Let us now review briefly a few of the
great and inescapable realities which
confront us in this post-modern age as
we "stand on the threshold of phase four
of history." Perhaps the greatest of them
all is the fact that the earth has become
a "little neighborhood" and is growing
smaller by the minute. As these words
are being written, Lieutenant Command-
er M. Scott Carpenter is orbiting the
planet at a speed of more than seventeen
thousand miles per hour. We have rocket
ships that can travel within the atmos-
phere at a rate of three to four thousand
miles per hour. And the miracle of Telstar
will doubtless enable every people to look

into the back yard of every other. Thus
the great cycle which opened in the Garden of Eden seven hundred thousand or
more years ago is closing in our time. How
large this legendary "garden" was where
man first appeared and ate of the fruit
of the tree of knowledge of good and evil
we do not know. But, in all likelihood, it
was in important respects smaller than
the entire earth is today. That Adam
could have stood at one end of the garden
and talked to Eve at the other or that
he could have walked across it in a single
day seems highly improbable. And so, in
a sense, we are back at the beginning of
the human adventure, but with a crucial
difference. From his place of origin, as
he developed his culture, he moved out
in all directions, conquered rivers, moun-
tains, deserts, seas, oceans, and climate;
and, in the course of time, took possession of practically the entire land surface of the globe. Today all of the races
and peoples and nations, all of the lan-
guages and cultures and religions and
social systems, with their accumulated
fears, hatreds, prejudices, and igno-

rances formed during the long period of
migration and conquest, are crowded together in this little earthly neighborhood.
Whether they can learn to live together
in peace, sympathy, friendship, and
brotherhood on this vastly shrunken
planet before they are all consumed in
an atomic holocaust when "time shall be
no more" is the supreme question confronting all mankind. As someone has
said, "distance has been annihilated, but
the *sense* of distance remains." Here
without doubt is a basic challenge to education in all countries and particularly
in the countries of the free world. The
minds of men will have to be changed
and prepared to face this basic reality
of the swiftly unfolding age.

The closing of this major cycle in human history has a very special meaning
for us in America. When Alexis de Tocqueville, the brilliant young French aris-
tocrat, arrived in the United States in
April, 1831, he was fundamentally hostile toward the idea of democracy and
feared that it might triumph in France
and the rest of Europe. Within a few

months, however, he gradually changed his mind and in September recorded in his notes "ten causes" for the relatively successful operation of our institutions. The second of these causes was: "Their geographical position. No neighbors." Unquestionably, the development of our democracy was profoundly influenced and greatly favored by the presence of the great oceans, east and west, which served as powerful bulwarks of freedom provided by nature. Today these oceans are gone, never to return! Consequently, every social, political, economic, military, or ideological storm that rises anywhere on the planet quickly reaches our shores. Moreover, an event occurring on the far side of the earth, such as the Japanese invasion of Manchuria in 1931 or the triumph of Communism in China in 1949, may prove to be more important for us in America than anything happening at the time within our own borders, even a presidential election. We have resisted most stubbornly the acceptance of the fact of the passing of the oceans and continue to experience a nostalgic longing for the condition of isolation which nurtured and guarded our bold experiment in the "cause of liberty" for three centuries. The doctrine of absolute sovereignty is already an anachronism and clearly some measure of the rule of law will have to be established on the earth. As Hans Kohn has stated recently in his *The Age of Nationalism,* "All preceding history has been parochial history. In the middle of the twentieth century mankind has entered the first stage of global history."

The second great reality of the age is closely linked with the first. A minor cycle embracing approximately five centuries is also closing in our time. If the fabled visitor from Mars had circled the earth on his flying saucer in the middle of the fifteenth century, he might well have concluded that the light-skinned peoples inhabiting the great peninsula jutting out from the Eurasian continent were in danger of being enslaved or driven into the sea. From time immemorial, with a few exceptions, the "hordes of Asia," the Magyars, the Bul-

gars, the Avars, the Khazars, the Pech-
enegs, the Polovtsy, the Tatars, and
others, had pressed upon them, ofttimes
with frightening success. In 1453 the
Tatars were still exacting tribute from
the Russian princes, the Moors were still
entrenched on the Iberian peninsula, and
the Ottoman Turks, having taken Con-
stantinople, were striking boldly and triumphantly at the southeastern gates of
Europe. Then, owing to a number of fac-
tors, including certainly the invention of
new weapons of warfare and the advance
of nautical science, the tables were
turned. The peoples of Europe went on
the offensive and moved out from their
limited domain. By the end of the nineteenth century they held nine-tenths of
the land surface of the globe, dominated
the remainder, and ruled the "seven
seas." As a result of their fabulous successes, they developed a sense of unqualified superiority and assumed that
they were destined by their very nature
to govern the world and rule the "lesser
breeds" of mankind. At the same time
they forced on all other peoples a sense

of inferiority. Today the colonial empires, with the exception of the Russian, founded in the epoch of European ascendancy are in process of complete disintegration and the so-called "colored peoples" are rising everywhere. That they will be satisfied with anything less than equality of status among the nations seems altogether improbable. And it must be realized that they constitute two-thirds of the human race.

In this situation our treatment of the Negro assumes a fateful urgency. Here is the greatest failure of our American democracy. Friendly visitors from other lands have remarked the contradiction between our moral commitments and our actions in this realm since colonial times. St. John de Crevecoeur, who lived with us for years before the War for Independence, wrote in one of his letters: "This great contrast has often afforded me most afflicting meditation." Tocqueville, George Combe, James Bryce, and many others expressed similar thoughts. In 1927 Andre Siegfried, noted French scholar and traveller, regarded "the colour problem as an abyss into which we can look only with terror." Concluded Gunnar Myrdal in 1944: "The simple fact is that an educational offensive against racial intolerance . . . has never been seriously attempted in America." We must realize that, with the closing of the great cycles, this is no longer a purely domestic question. It corrupts the "image of America" and the "Voice of America" from Tokyo to New Delhi, to Cairo, to Leopoldville, to Rio, to the halls of the United Nations. It is no defense to point to the delinquencies of other nations. We should never forget that we wrote and adopted the Declaration of Independence and that, consequently, more is expected of us. We should never forget also that the United States, because of its traditions and its great power, is the leader of the free nations. Our failures in the realm of race relations, therefore, may cause us to lose the great struggle for human freedom in the world. Every such failure is grasped eagerly by our adversary in the Kremlin and, in exaggerated form, joined with a measure of hypocrisy, broadcast to every corner of the globe. Here is a major challenge to American education. And history does not wait. How fortunate would we be today if the name, "American Negro," were carried with pride to all the continents!

The closing of these two cycles has been attended by a fabulous increase in the power reposing in the hands of man—power which opens unlimited vistas for good or evil. There is, first of all, power over the forces of nature. In the technically advanced countries human muscle provides but the tiniest fraction of the energy employed in the production of goods and services and the maintenance of the vast systems of communication and transportation. And with the coming of automation, the role of the human brain will be profoundly altered. Also the ancient relation between labor and leisure will be reversed. There is, secondly, power over human life and death. Most of the dread diseases of the past can now be banished from the earth, the birth-rate can be controlled, and the life span can be extended far beyond the dreams of earlier ages, or even of this age. Man also possesses the means for destroying himself utterly and bringing to a close his entire adventure on the earth. At the same time, human fertility, the powerful urge to reproduce, if unregulated, may cause a political explosion as devastating as that of the atomic bomb. Finally, there is power over the human mind. Through the new weapons of warfare, the swift means of transportation, and the fantastic media of mass communication, combined with advances in the psychological sciences, a tiny, disciplined, and ruthless minority is now able to enslave whole nations and shape the minds of millions according to the desired pattern. It is this development that distinguishes the contemporary totalitarian state from the despotisms of the past. May we not even say that totalitarianism, like the atomic bomb, is one of the triumphs of science and technology? And in the biological sciences we seem to be approaching the time when we will be able to create living things

and shape the nature of man according
to our desires. The crucial question here,
of course, is: Given the present level of
his morals, what will man do with all of
this fabulous power? The answer is far
from clear today.

Although the earthly neighborhood is
fantastically small when measured in
terms of speed of communication, it is
vast indeed when viewed from the standpoint of human understanding. This
brings us to a fourth great reality.
Science and technology have created a
system of national and world relationships so wide in its sweep, so complex in
its patterns, and so dynamic in its tendencies that the thoughtful mind must
wonder whether its control may not be
beyond the power of its creator. Here is
the intellectual challenge of the new age
—a challenge to our democracy and to
our education. Our political system seems
to be founded on the presupposition that
the ordinary man or woman not only can,
but will, acquire the knowledge and understanding necessary to enable him or
her to pass informed judgment on great

issues of policy and on personalities. And it is in this realm that democracy is challenged by Communism and other totalitarian systems under which all political decisions are made by an "elite." Many years ago, when the task was much simpler than it is today, Walter Lippmann in his *The Phantom Public* wrote: "Although public business is my main interest and I give most of my time to watching it, I cannot find time to do what is expected of me in the theory of democracy; that is, to know what is going on and to have an opinion worth expressing on every question which confronts a self-governing community." And Tocqueville, contemplating our democracy in the simple agrarian age, concluded that "a democracy is unable to regulate the details of an important undertaking, to persevere in a design, and to work out its execution in the presence of serious obstacles." The dynamism of the contemporary world adds greatly to the task confronting a self-governing community, for when we think we have arrived at understanding, the configuration of forces and events may suddenly undergo radical transformation. And what are we to say about that time, perhaps not too far distant, when the human race launches full-scaled explorations into the cosmos!

A fifth great reality is the profound change in the power structure of the world. When the last bomb exploded in the Second World War it was evident that the center of gravity of industrial, military, and political power had shifted from the base on which it had rested for several centuries. It had shifted from Western Europe to the east and to the west—to the Soviet Union and to the United States of America. Thus, the extraordinary prediction of Alexis de Tocqueville in 1835 was fulfilled. In the closing chapter of the first volume of his *Democracy in America,* he turns his thoughts to the futures of these two countries. "There are at the present time," he writes, "two great nations in the world, which started from different points, but seem to tend towards the same end. I allude to the Russians and the Americans." Then, after contrasting these two peoples in terms that would apply today, he concludes as follows: "Their starting points are different, and their courses are not the same; yet, each of them seems marked out by the will of Heaven to sway the destinies of half the globe." A personal letter from Charles A. Beard, dated July 13, 1945, before the war was over in the East, closed with these words: "The sky is clear and ominous: only two mighty armed powers are on the horizon. What impends and with what portents? Day and night, I wonder and tremble for the future of my country and mankind." The letter was written a year before the beginning of the "Cold War," when some of our citizens were referring to Russia as "our great democratic ally" and the American people generally, according to the opinion polls, were quite optimistic about our future relations with the Soviet Union. However, we must realize that the present power pattern is certain to change in the coming years. A United States of Europe is a clear possibility and Communist

China looms on the horizon, with what "portents" we do not know.

This brings us to the last of the great realities to be listed here. From the standpoint of the "preservation of the sacred fire of liberty" in the world Communism may well prove to be the most challenging of the great realities of the sixties and after. The dynamism and sweep of this movement in forty-five years surpass all of its rivals of the past. No other religious or political system, or body of doctrine, ever advanced so swiftly and so far in a single generation. Launched in 1917 by Lenin and his 240,000 members of the Party of Bolsheviks, it established its rule over practically the entire territory of the Russian Empire, the "sixth continent," or "one-sixth of the land surface of the globe." Then, following the "Great Patriotic War," as the Second World War is called in the Soviet Union, it moved west and east to embrace one-third of the people of the earth. Four years ago a leading Soviet educator presented the official Soviet view at the time in these apocalyptic terms : "The mighty ideas of a new world born of the great October Revolution are winning triumphantly the minds and the hearts of millions of people. Marching with the one billion population of the socialist countries are approximately seven hundred million people in former colonial countries which have achieved their independence and six hundred million in lands now struggling for independence. There remain in the countries of the camp of imperialism only about four hundred million. Today, as picturesquely expressed by Mao Tse Tung, 'It is no longer the West wind that directs the East wind, but the East wind that directs the West wind.' " We may smile at this boastful pronouncement, but it would probably be the counsel of wisdom to view it seriously and to strive with all our energy to strengthen the heritage of freedom. For the first time in our history we are being challenged by a powerful and resourceful rival for the hopes and affections of the oppressed and exploited peoples of the earth. And it should be noted

that the Twenty-Second Congress of the
Communist Party of the Soviet Union,
meeting in October, 1961, issued a great
slogan which constitutes a mighty effort
to appropriate the ideas of the American and French revolutions: "Hail Communism, Assuring on the Earth Peace,
Labor, Liberty, Equality, Fraternity,
and Happiness for all Peoples." This
slogan is being propagated with all the
power of the Communist apparatus at
home and throughout the world, and, especially, among the former colonial peoples. One of the anomalies of the age is
the fact that a ruthless dictatorship pre-
sents itself, probably with some success,
as the champion of liberty. The accusing
finger is pointing squarely at the substance of education in America and the
other countries of the free world.

THE ROLE OF EDUCATION

We in America have an enviable record in the history of education. From
early colonial times we have cherished
the school and have identified education
with the advance of civilization. Even

as we struggled to survive in a strange and often hostile land we nurtured this faith. The founders of the Republic, under the influence of the revolutionary thought of the age in both Europe and America, believed that the strength of the new nation would depend on the spread of learning and enlightenment. "If the condition of man is to be progressively ameliorated," wrote Thomas Jefferson, father of American democracy, in 1818, "education is to be the chief instrument in effecting it." The foremost champions of popular liberty throughout our national history have generally insisted that the survival of free institutions requires an educated people. Horace Mann, father of the common school, expressed the sentiments of generations of Americans when he said: "The Common School is the greatest discovery ever made by man." When confronted with difficult personal or social problems in the present critical epoch, we are inclined to turn to education as an unfailing solution. Equally, when something goes wrong, we are inclined to blame education. And by education we commonly mean what goes on in the school. According to this faith, only free societies will establish and support schools for the many, because despotisms and autocracies want "to keep their peoples in ignorance."

In *The Outline of History,* published in 1920, H. G. Wells, one of the prophets of the early twentieth century, declared that "human history becomes more and more a race between education and catastrophe." During the nineteen-twenties this statement was probably quoted more frequently at educational meetings in the United States than any other. It was clearly in accord with our traditional faith. Early in 1939, in his *The Fate of Man,* Wells gloomily observed that catastrophe was "well on its way," that education seemed "unable to get started," that "indeed it had not readjusted itself to start." He concluded with the dismal thought that "the race may, after all, prove a walk-over for disaster."

We know today that catastrophe triumphed, and with terrifying swiftness. Yet, that it had been a race between education and catastrophe is true only with qualifications, as Wells himself would have been among the first to admit. The years between the wars witnessed an unprecedented expansion of organized education, of schools and colleges and many other agencies for the molding and the informing of the minds of both young and old. In fact, never before in the history of man had the problem of rearing the young and instructing the old received so much attention from the heads of government and the leaders of society. Here in the United States the number of students attending secondary schools increased from 2,500,000 in 1920 to 6,925,000 in 1940, while the enrollment in higher schools advanced from 750,000 to 1,800,000. During the same period Soviet Russia probably directed a larger *proportion* of the total national income to the support of education than any other country in history. The number of young and old attending schools and classes of all grades and types advanced from eight or nine millions to perhaps thirty-five or forty millions. Following the Revolution and particularly after launching the First Five-Year Plan in 1928, the Soviet leaders conducted the most comprehensive campaign ever attempted anywhere to "liquidate" illiteracy. And the entire cultural apparatus, including the press, the radio, the movie, the theatre, and even the circus, were directed toward the achievement of clearly and explicitly formulated distant social and educational goals. The Axis powers—Germany, Italy and Japan —spent enormous sums and vast energies on education and gave as close attention to shaping the minds of children and youth as to the building of the economy and the strengthening of the armed forces. In many other countries it was also an era of educational expansion. Consequently, the youth of 1939 was the most schooled generation in history. Clearly, if our traditional faith in the school is sound, the Second World War did not happen.

The fact, of course, is that the race was not between education and catastrophe, unless one wants to define the term in a very special way. In large measure, education was actually the handmaiden or midwife of catastrophe, as it has often been through the ages. This was obviously and avowedly true in the case of all the totalitarian states. Children were taught in Fascist Italy that the time had come to restore the glories of the Roman Empire, that "it is better to live a day as a lion than a thousand years as a lamb"; in Nazi Germany, that the Nordic race is immeasurably superior to all others, that the soil of the Ukraine, the minerals of the Urals, and the forests of Siberia should really belong to the Third Reich, that only in war does man fulfill his highest destiny; in Japan under the military caste, that the Japanese are the chosen people of God, that they should rightly covet the orange groves of California, that death in battle for the glory of the Son of Heaven is the most exalted purpose in life. In the Soviet Union the schools were employed to foster the class struggle, to falsify history and misrepresent the institutions of other nations, and to propagate the doctrine that Russia was the spearhead of a world revolution which in time would spread to all countries and overthrow the existing social order everywhere. At the same time no free society anywhere confronted the problem boldly and imaginatively. In the United States educational agencies, besides teaching by example, if not by precept, the superiority of the white race and the sanctity of the system of private capitalism, were busily engaged in preparing the young to struggle for individual material success and to live in a world that had passed away. Throughout the earth, education, either deliberately or unwittingly, helped to bring upon mankind the disasters that all but destroyed the best in our civilization. At the very least, it was not designed, either in conception or in practice, to oppose the swift advance of catastrophe.

Our traditional faith in organized education rests on two assumptions: first, that it is powerful; and, second, that it is beneficent. The first is unquestionably correct and has been proved to be so in our time by the totalitarian states. That it is beneficent in the sense that it always promotes human freedom and popular government is obviously incorrect. Aristotle observed that there is "an appropriate form of education ... for every state." Montesquieu in his great classic, *Spirit of the Laws,* read and pondered by the founders of our Republic, wrote that "the laws of education ought to be in relation to the principles of government." And in his Ninth Annual Report in 1845 Horace Mann stated the principle with his usual clarity of expression: "If there are no two things wider asunder than freedom and slavery, then must the course of training which fits children for these two opposite conditions be as diverse as the points to which they lead."

All human experience demonstrates that education in any living society is never neutral. It is not enough, therefore, to say we need more and more education, as if it were an autonomous process governed by its own laws and dedicated to human freedom. We must abandon completely the naive faith that the school automatically liberates the mind and serves the cause of human progress. In fact, we know that it may serve any cause, that it may serve tyranny as well as freedom, ignorance as well as enlightenment, falsehood as well as truth, war as well as peace, death as well as life. It may lead men and women to think they are free even as it rivets upon them the chains of bondage. Education is indeed a force of great power, particularly when the word is made to embrace all of the agencies and organized processes for molding the mind, but whether it is good or evil depends, not on the laws of learning, but on the conception of life and civilization which gives it substance and direction. In the course of history education has served every purpose and doctrine contrived by man. If it is to serve the cause of human freedom, it must be explicitly designed for that purpose. We must know also that literacy cannot be a liberating force for the popular masses in the absence of a free press.

The commitment to human freedom is a great faith which, in its origins, can be traced back through the ages to ancient times. In the course of its history, it has experienced many advances and retreats, many triumphs and defeats, as J. B. Bury has demonstrated. And it stands in great peril today. The essence of this faith is that only under freedom can man grow to his full intellectual, moral, artistic, and spiritual stature. But freedom assumes many different forms in human societies and cultures. It includes freedom of the mind, freedom of conscience, freedom of expression, freedom of movement, freedom of occupation, freedom of association, and freedom of political action. In his comprehensive *Freedom and Civilization* Malinowski writes: "Although political freedom is not the only type of freedom in culture, yet its absence destroys all other liberties." He consequently observes that "at present the battle of freedom is fought between the two principles, that of democracy and of totalitarianism." The present lecture, being based on this analysis of the nature of human freedom, will confine itself for the most part to the foundations of political liberty. We can scarcely speak of free men under a despotism.

The present condition of man calls for nothing less than a supreme effort in the field of education, even in America. And here we must emphasize that men are not born free, nor is their freedom ordained by the laws of God or nature. On the contrary men are born, neither bound nor free, but helpless and endowed with almost infinite possibilities for good or evil. A society of free men is perhaps the highest achievement of the race, and also perhaps the most difficult to establish and sustain over a period of time. The author of the Declaration of Independence, near the end of his life, stated the principle here with utmost clarity: "The qualifications for self-government in society are not innate. They are the result of habit and long training." And Herbert Spencer, in his essay on "The Americans" in 1892, put his thoughts in these words: "The Republican form of government is the highest form of government; but because of this it requires the highest form of human nature—a type nowhere at present existing." Edmund Burke, a century earlier, arrived at a similar conclusion. Of the three forms of government in history, despotism, aristocracy, and republic, the first, he said, being "the simplest form of government is infinitely the most general." As we have noted above, education will serve the cause of liberty only if it is designed to do so. This means that it must strive to build the foundations of liberty in the institutions of society and in the minds and hearts of the members of the younger generation—a stupendous and arduous task.

THE TANGIBLE SUPPORTS OF LIBERTY

The foundations of political liberty are both tangible and intangible, although it is difficult to separate the two. Every tangible support will be found to have intangible aspects. This truth is perhaps most easily demonstrated in the rule of law which Sir Ernest Barker has called "*the* foundation of foundations" of the

Western political tradition. Although
laws may be unwritten, we commonly
think of them as enacted by some legislative body at some particular time and
printed in our statute books. Also there
are the police and the courts. Where laws
govern the governors, as well as ordinary
citizens, we have perhaps the most indispensable support of human freedom.
"The Habeaus Corpus Act," wrote Lord
Macaulay in 1889, "is the most stringent
curb that ever legislation imposed on
tyranny." If by some strange psychological cataclysm we were to lose our entire
heritage of law with its associated habits, knowledges, and attitudes, its institutions and philosophical conceptions,
our political system and way of life
would pass into swift dissolution. Unfor-
tunately men who live under the rule of
law commonly have little appreciation of
its worth and accept it unconsciously as
a part of the order of nature, and perhaps to be evaded when possible. Only
when it is interrupted or destroyed in
some great social convulsion and the individual is confronted on all sides by the

rule of unrestrained caprice and naked
force do men fully sense its meaning and
value. As R. M. MacIver has said, "Without law there is no order, and without
order men are lost, not knowing where
they go, not knowing what they do." And
without law there can be no freedom,
except the freedom of the jungle, and
no justice. Inculcation of "love of the
laws", therefore, is the most fundamental task of education in a free society.
This embraces, of course, love of the laws
under which the laws themselves may
be changed. And such conditioning cannot begin too early in the life of the
individual.

Of the tangible supports of liberty,
power would seem to be most important.
In fact freedom without power in some
form for either the individual or the
group has no meaning. The significance
of this question has been recognized
since ancient times. More than two thousand year ago Thucydides, the Greek
historian, has one of his characters say:
"We both alike know that into the discussion of human affairs the question of

justice only enters where the pressure of necessity is equal, and that the powerful exact what they can, and the weak grant what they must." And liberty without justice is not liberty. Perhaps the most famous formulation of the question is the aphorism of Lord Acton, an aphorism that has gone around the world: "Power tends to corrupt and absolute power corrupts absolutely." Although intangible forces have been known to soften this harsh judgment of human nature, our experience with the totalitarian dictators in this century has dramatically supported the judgment of the great English student of freedom and power. But we should realize that the tendency of power to corrupt applies to groups, classes, nations, and races, as well as to individuals. This principle is illustrated, as we have seen, in the sweep of European imperialism from the fifteenth century and the enslaving of the Negro in America and other countries. Power, of course, appears in different forms which will now be briefly reviewed.

We in America have been inclined to think of power in political terms. And here we have an enviable record. Beginning with severe property qualifications immediately following the launching of the Republic, we moved during the generations to universal white manhood suffrage and after the Civil War to the announced extension of full voting rights to male Negroes. Finally, with the adoption of the Nineteenth Amendment to the Federal Constitution in 1919, we guaranteed to all women the right of suffrage and thus established *in the law* the principle of equal and universal participation in the exercise of political power. However, we all know that there remain millions of people who, by reason of race, economic condition, or cultural deprivation, remain "second-class citizens" in this land of liberty and plenty. This fact, so contrary to our professions, must be eternally on the conscience of every person who professes devotion to the cause of human freedom. The founding fathers, moreover, being students of the history of political institutions and keenly aware of the dangers inherent in the concentration of power, provided in the Constitution for the separation of powers through three coordinate branches of government—the executive, the legislature, and the judiciary. The question today, as we face the sweep, the complexity, and the dynamism of human society, is whether the ordinary voter is equipped with the knowledge, the wisdom, and the dedication to freedom essential to the exercise of his sacred right to shape the destinies of the Republic.

A second form of power, which has been recognized by all students of government through the ages, is economic. "When the rich grow numerous or properties increase," Aristotle observed, "the form of government changes into an oligarchy or a government of families." Alexander Hamilton, arguing for a "fixed provision" for the support of judges in the seventy-ninth number of the *Federalist,* stated the principle with utter clarity: "In the general course of human nature, a power over a man's subsistence amounts to power over his will."

And Daniel Webster declared at the Massachusetts Constitutional Convention in 1820: "It seems to me to be plain, that, in the absence of military force, political power naturally and necessarily goes into the hands which hold the property. In my judgment, therefore, a republican form of government rests not more on political constitutions than on those laws which regulate the descent and transmission of property." We must realize today that the economic base of American politics bears little resemblance to the situation which so impressed Alexis de Tocqueville in 1831—"the general equality of condition among the people." One need not accept in all of its details and implications the thesis of C. Wright Mills regarding the "corporate rich" in his *The Power Elite* to sense the presence of a danger to our liberties in the realm of economic affairs. However, we must note that this form of power is no longer confined to the ownership of property. The heads of our great labor organizations, enrolling some fifteen million working men and women, have at their command tremendous economic power, sufficient to paralyze the economy. And Adolf A. Berle has demonstrated conclusively in his *Power without Property* that in our great corporations power tends to go into the hands, not of the owners of stocks, but of a new elite, product of the advance of technology, the managerial class. Moreover, according to his analysis, "some five hundred great corporations dominate through outright ownership two-thirds of the industry of the United States." Any program of education for human freedom must focus its eyes anxiously in this direction.

Probably the most decisive form of power in the history of society, as Daniel Webster implied, is military force. In the early years of this century, before the rise of totalitarian movements and systems, there was a general tendency on the part of students of politics to emphasize economic rather than military power, probably on the assumption that the exercise of the latter had passed into history. The generation of the founding fathers, however, realized fully the importance of keeping military power in the hands of the people. They abolished the military caste, made the military subordinate to the civil authority, and thus erected one of the most powerful defenses of liberty in the political history of the human race. Also they inserted as the second article of the Bill of Rights the provision that the "right of the people to keep and bear arms shall not be infringed." They were aware that the development of the spirit of liberty in colonial times was profoundly influenced by the wide distribution of military force among the people, exemplified by the "long rifle," the most precise and deadly weapon man had ever invented, hanging over the fireplace. With the improvement of weapons and the westward migration of our people the idea seems to have developed that the principle of equality rested in some measure on the firearm. The following couplet, it is recorded, may be found on some old Colt revolvers, first patented in 1836: "Be not afraid of any man, no matter what his size. When danger threatens, call on me, and I will

equalize." Sometimes the same thought
was expressed thus: "It wasn't God or
the Declaration of Independence that
made all men free and equal; it was Col-
onel Sam'l Colt." Another version was:
"All men are not born equal—Sam'l Colt
made 'em that way." And Thomas Car-
lyle once said: "Gunpowder has made
men all of one height." But it must be
recognized that the Second Amendment
has been repealed, not by political action,
but by the advance of military technology. We should heed the warning in President Eisenhower's farewell address on
January 17, 1961: "This conjunction of
an immense military establishment and
a large arms industry is new in the
American experience. The total influence
—economic, political, even spiritual—is
felt in every city, every statehouse, every
office of the federal government. . . . We
must never let the weight of this combination endanger our liberties or democratic processes." The foundations of
human freedom have indeed been profoundly transformed in this age of science and technology.

There are, of course, other forms of power which should be mentioned. There is the power resident in a rigid class structure which has characterized most societies in history—a form of power which grants and limits opportunities of all kinds and which molds the minds of both the high- and the low-born, but which generally, though not absent, has been weaker in America than in other countries because of the factor of social mobility. Then there is ecclesiastical power which reaches its climax in the state church. From this threat to popular liberty we have had little to fear. We are protected by the first article of the Bill of Rights, and by the facts of life. We are most fortunate in that we have not just one church, but approximately two hundred and fifty religious sects. Consequently, there is no single authority capable of proclaiming and imposing the "one truth" in the realm of religion and morals. Finally, there is the power of the voluntary organization. Here we find the dynamics of American politics which so impressed Alexis de Tocqueville.

Having seen nothing comparable in the Europe of his day, he said: "Americans of all ages, and all conditions, constantly form associations. They have not only commercial and manufacturing companies, in which all take part, but associations of a thousand other kinds—religious, moral, serious, futile, general or restricted, enormous or diminutive." And he linked this practice with our political liberties: "There is only one country (America) on the face of the earth where the citizens enjoy unlimited freedom of association for political purposes." The truth of his observation has been demonstrated time and again in this century by the totalitarian movements. Among the first acts of the totalitarian on seizing power is to abolish or "coordinate," meaning control, all voluntary associations. However, there is a large and crucial educational task confronting us here. Many of these associations are dedicated to the advancement of the selfish interests of their members. The general welfare, which should be paramount, is neglected.

Another broad tangible support of freedom is a general condition of security. Our geographical position behind the great oceans, which now are gone, was a factor of great importance for three centuries. Economic security, as we well know from experience, is basic to the operation of free institutions. It was no historical accident that Mussolini came to power during the first economic depression following the First World War or that Hitler overthrew the Weimar Republic during the second. Also in a democracy the efficient operation of political institutions is essential to survival. Mussolini characterized a parliament as a "debating society." It just could not do the things that had to be done. In the measure that our legislative bodies resort to delays and filibusters to block needed legislative action, they undermine and weaken popular faith in our constitutional system. Only a people sensitive to the general welfare and eternally watchful can correct these tendencies. Here our press and other media of mass communication must play a major and responsible role.

THE INTANGIBLE SUPPORTS OF LIBERTY

We come now to the intangible supports of liberty. And it is here that education, involving not only the school but also all of the agencies for molding and informing the mind, must make the major contribution. The question has often been asked: Why do men obey the laws? While the obvious answer leads to the police, the courts, and fear of punishment for infractions, the analysis must go behind and beneath the laws to the character of a people and into the realm of traditions, habits, values, and loyalties. Laws do not enforce themselves. And it has been truly said that "liberty descends from precedent to precedent."

The problem here is clearly presented by Walton Hamilton in his article on "Constitutionalism" in the *Encyclopedia of the Social Sciences:* "The rise of constitutionalism may be dated from 1776. . . . From the two revolutionary centers of the United States and France the contagion has spread throughout the Americas, continental Europe, Australia, South Africa, and even the Orient. In a century and a half a count of instruments in which peoples have embodied their faith runs into hundreds." Yet, only a handful have survived. The constitution of the Weimar Republic was often characterized in the nineteen-twenties as a product of the most advanced political thought, formally superior in many respects to the constitutions of the preceding century and a half. Yet it failed to halt the rise of despotism and the establishment of a dictatorship in Germany by "constitutional" means. In divers countries governments resting on excellent written constitutions have been overthrown periodically by strong, ruthless, and ambitious men. Thus, according to Feliks Gross, in his *The Seizure of Political Power,* "Bolivia had 178 revolutionary or violent changes of the government, from the time of its independence in 1825 to 1952."

Even under the best of constitutions there will come times of crisis when vast power—power sufficient to destroy the law—will be lodged in the hands of a few men. What is it in these situations that holds power in leash? What is it that persuades the sword to "sheathe itself," to employ an expression from a bygone age? Such questions are not easily answered. Obviously men who at a given moment have at their command overwhelming military force are scarcely restrained by fear of arrest, imprisonment, or execution. Arthur Balfour, a distinguished English statesman and political philosopher, addresses himself to this question in his introduction to the World's Classics edition of Walter Bagehot's *The English Constitution* in 1928. "Could it," he asks, "long survive the shocks of revolutionary and counter-revolutionary violence?" And he answers: "I know not. The experiment has never been tried. Our Alternating Cabinets, though belonging to different Parties, have never differed about the foundations of society." He then proceeds to enumerate the qualities of mind and heart essential to the survival of the constitution in case the basic issues are ever raised, as they were in August, 1945. Here are his wise words which should serve as a guide for any education designed to serve the cause of freedom under law:

> It matters little what other gifts a people may possess if they are wanting in those which, from this point of view are of most importance . . . If, for example, they have no capacity for grading their loyalties as well as for being moved by them; if they have no natural inclination to liberty and no natural respect for law; if they lack good humour and tolerate foul play; if they know not how to compromise or when; if they have not that distrust of extreme conclusions which is sometimes misdescribed as want of logic; if corruption does not repel them; and if their divisions tend to be either too numerous or too profound, the successful working of British institutions may be difficult if not impossible.

This excellent statement from a distinguished representative of a people who in the course of centuries contributed more than any other to the building of the foundations of liberty in the modern world, a people to whom we have been profoundly indebted from the days of the earliest colonial settlements, may serve

as a point of departure in the review of
those intangibles, those moral and spiritual qualities, without which institutional expressions of human freedom would
wither and die. This will take us into the
realm of values, the most neglected as-
pect of our educational endeavor. The
time has long since arrived when we
must ask ourselves in all seriousness:
What are the basic values, the fundamental loyalties and moral commitments,
on which a truly free society rests? For
there is an essential morality for every
social and political system or way of life.
If that morality decays or is taken for
granted as a gift from nature, the system itself will pass into history to be
studied in some future age by scholars
working in the social sciences. An education that assumes an agnostic posture on
this issue, pursues a policy of *laissez
faire,* or leaves all decisions to chance or
the child is utterly unrealistic and Uto-
pian. As a matter of fact, it is quite impossible to launch and operate a school or
any other educational agency without
making a thousand choices positively in-

volving values, from the architecture of a building, to the materials in a textbook, to the personality of a teacher. Our first responsibility is to know, in so far as possible, what we are doing. There is no escape under the aegis of rescuing the child from the ogre of indoctrination.

First of all, we should strive through the entire educational program, through the curriculum and the extracurricular activities, through the social relations of teachers and pupils, of pupils with pupils, of teachers with administrators, and of the school with parents and the community to inculcate a deep love of liberty. The members of the younger generation should become familiar with the long struggle for freedom, not only in the history of our people, but also in the history of mankind. They should know the story as told in that monumental work of James T. Shotwell, *The Long Way to Freedom*, in which one of our most distinguished scholars traces the struggle for liberty from earliest times, recording the many advances and retreats, successes and failures along the

way, and portraying the contending
forces in the present troubled age. The
great objective here, moreover, would be
to regard the liberties enjoyed in our society, not simply as a heritage from the
past, but as a legacy to be guarded jeal-
ously and transmitted to the next generation in an enriched and strengthened condition. The Bill of Rights, with its priceless guarantees to all, should be regarded
as a sacred document. We must recognize
that, in the words of one of our most
famous judges, Learned Hand, "Liberty
lies in the hearts of men and women;
when it dies there, no constitution, no
law, no court can save it; no constitution,
no law, no court can even do much to
help it." Only through the processes of
tuition and learning, whether in school
or out, can the love of liberty be made to
lie "in the hearts of men and women." As
we have already noted, members of the
human species are not born with a devotion to political liberty. On the contrary,
it is one of the noblest achievements of
the race, an achievement which may be
easily corrupted and lost. In these days

we should heed the warning of James Harvey Robinson more than a generation ago: "How precarious are the finest achievements of the human spirit!"

Underlying the tradition of liberty is a profound moral commitment which we in the West derive from the Judaeo-Christian ethic. This ethic proclaims, without qualification, the supreme worth and dignity of the individual human being. Every man is precious simply because he is a man. Every man is precious also because he is unique, because he is himself and no other. Here, then, is the source of all values. The development of the individual to his full stature, physical, intellectual, moral, aesthetic, and spiritual, is the purpose and the gauge of human society and relationships. As the founder of Christianity once observed, even the Sabbath was made for man, and not man for the Sabbath. So all institutions and social arrangements—family and neighborhood; industry, state, and church; social, economic, and political systems; religions and moral codes; press, radio, and television; the movie, the theatre, music, and art; yes, even schools and colleges—are to be judged, accepted, or rejected, preserved or modified, as they affect the lives of individual human beings. This recognition of the supreme worth of the individual leads inevitably to the principle of equality among the members of society. If each individual is uniquely precious, there can be no moral support for privileged orders and castes. No man can be regarded as superior or inferior to another by reason of the work he does, the social rank of his family, the color of his skin, or even the altar at which he worships. Nor for any reason whatsoever does any man have the right to exploit another, to use another as a means to his ends. Failure to honor this basic moral principle of the worth and dignity of the individual leads inevitably to the denial of the blessings of liberty to millions of "citizens" and places in jeopardy the tradition of freedom itself.

The development in the members of the younger generation of deep commitment and loyalty to this sublime principle should be recognized as a basic responsibility from the earliest years. One, of course, can only weep when he considers the severe and continuing violation of the principle in the case of the children of Negro stock, of migrant workers, of dwellers in the slums and culturally deprived areas. Yet, the school can do much to improve the condition through the equal and loving treatment of every child regardless of family, race, or creed, and by the encouragement of the pupil to live according to our political and ethical professions. It is in this connection that we as a people should renew our faith in the "common school." In the current controversy over federal aid to education, few of the spokesmen on either side seem to comprehend the issue. The private school, whether sectarian or aristocratic, is often defended on the ground that it is carrying a certain share of the load in the education of the younger generation and, therefore, should receive public support. This view betrays a profound failure to understand the nature of the "common school" and its role in our democracy. Why did Horace

Mann proclaim that "The Common School is the greatest discovery ever made by man"? Certainly not because it taught the so-called "common branches," nor because it provided educational opportunities for the "common people," but rather because in its perfected form it brings into close association in work and play the children of all elements of the population. In this association, under appropriate guidance, they may learn to respect one another and thus achieve a moral education appropriate to a democratic society. In my opinion, there is no substitute for the "common school." It constitutes one of the most glorious and distinctive achievements of our people and should be ranked alongside our system of democratic constitutional government of which it is an indispensable support. All elements of society should rally to its support and improvement.

A third of the intangible supports of liberty is toleration of and respect for differences—differences of opinion and thought. We may go even farther and say that differences should be valued and encouraged. Where men are free they will differ. And their differences are essential to the creative process in society and in life. The expression of a contrary point of view, even though founded on error, serves as a challenge to the accepted ways. But a contrary point of view may be founded on truth and thus serve to advance the cause of man. And one can never be certain in the absence of testing whether it is founded on truth or error. The history of human progress in all spheres of endeavor reveals the sobering fact that the initiators of change are almost invariably subjected to criticism and persecution. Many have been nailed to the cross or burned at the stake. This suggests that the "right to make mistakes" is one of the most precious rights of free men. Though not specifically guaranteed in our Bill of Rights, it is certainly implied in the First Amendment and in our entire system of constitutional government. To think or to venture is always to run the risk of error. But to be paralyzed by the fear of error is to repudiate that gift for creation which has lifted humankind from savagery. Only those who follow a life of complete routine or submission to authority are secure from "mistakes," and perhaps in pursuing this course they commit the greatest mistake of all. Consequently, the rights of minorities must be zealously guarded in a free society. At the same time, the expression of differences must proceed in the spirit of respect for and obedience to the laws. The alternative is anarchy and the end of freedom.

A closely related support of liberty is the encouragement of the critical mind. Here we encounter the long tradition of authoritarianism which has generally characterized organized education since ancient times. The school has its teachers, courses of study, and textbooks, which supposedly represent revealed truth and are, therefore, to be accepted on faith. The pupil is commonly expected to regard this revelation as standing above and beyond doubt or criticism. But something more must be said. The youngster should not be encouraged to engage in criticism just for the sake of criticism. The truly critical mind is one of the most precious resources of a free society. At the same time such a mind must be highly disciplined. It must be armed with knowledge and understanding, and perhaps with a modicum of humility and wisdom. The great scientist working in his field of specialization must even view the accepted "laws" of his science with a measure of doubt. But to do so effectively he must undergo and practice a severe discipline, perhaps more severe than that found in any other realm of human activity. He must follow a rigorous and austere code. He must practice the intellectual virtues of accuracy, precision, truthfulness, open-mindedness, and absolute integrity. If he is ignorant of the work of his colleagues, if he is careless in the keeping of his records, if he permits the passions of partisanship to influence his operations, if he allows his hopes and fears to warp either his observations or his generalizations, if he tempers his conclusions to appease the wrath of either constituted or unconstituted authorities, if he clings to an untenable hypothesis in the face of contrary evidence, if he conceals from his colleagues or from the public relevant facts concerning either his methods or his findings—in a word, if he allows himself to be controlled by any consideration except the disinterested pursuit and promulgation of truth, he is not a scientist. Here is one of the most precious traditions of mankind. It should be cultivated in all departments of education and of life.

Our system of political liberty, as we have noted, rests on the presupposition that the ordinary citizen can and will acquire the knowledge and understanding necessary for him to pass informed judgment on great issues of policy and on personalities. This means that the education of a free man must place great emphasis on relevant knowledge and understanding. Here we are victimized by our long tradition of anti-intellectualism. In some quarters the suggestion that our schools and colleges should attach as high social prestige to intellectual excellence as to athletic prowess would be regarded as subversive of the "American Way of Life." Often we hear knowledge dismissed as "mere knowledge." Yet again and again in this twentieth century we have witnessed peoples with a measure of liberty follow dictators and establish totalitarian regimes. It seems quite probable that they didn't really know what they were doing. Knowledge itself is one of the most basic forms of power. Clearly, if the cause of freedom is to triumph in the great struggle with despotism in the coming years and decades, the intellectual stature of our citizens must be radically increased. Our educational institutions must, first of all, convey to the younger generation an understanding of our political system and the foundations of human freedom. But they must do much more. They must reconstruct their curricula for the purpose of illuminating the nature of the world in which we are living and must live. We must study the great challenges of the age: the challenge of world Communism and other forms of totalitarianism, the challenge of the closing of the great cycles of history, the challenge of the decline of the West and the rise of non-European peoples, the challenge of the annihilation of distance and the reduction of the earth to the dimensions of a little neighborhood, the challenge of outer space and the penetration of the cosmos, the challenge of the fabulous power placed in man's hands, the challenge of the complexity and dynamism of society and culture, the challenge of science and technology, the challenge of change. This means, moreover, that a central purpose of education should be the development of a thirst for knowledge and understanding which would endure to the end of life.

This suggests that science should be studied from two different perspectives in our schools. On the one hand, appropriately gifted youth should be encouraged to study science in its many branches with the purpose of becoming scientists. On the other hand, all youth should study science as a basic humanistic subject, as a great ingredient of the culture, as the most powerful force moving in the modern world—a force that is daily changing our ways of life, our outlook on the universe, and our very conception of the nature and destiny of man. Because of our failure in terms of this second perspective, our minds continue to dwell in a world that has passed away. We should know that the scientific laboratory is the most radical of our institutions.

Coeval with knowledge and understanding as an intangible support of liberty is integrity in the entire political process. Francis Lieber, a distinguished American citizen and historian of German origin, published a two-volume work in 1835, *The Stranger in America.* In this work he describes an election in the United States in these words:

> I have stood on the evening of the 18th on the battlefield of Waterloo, when, as one of my company said, "the fun was o'er," and made my Hamlet contemplations, which forced themselves even on the mind of a lad; but nothing equals, I think, a morning after a closely contested election in a populous city. Rise early on the morning after and walk through the quiet streets. Walls and corners

are yet covered with flaming handbills, witnesses and documents of the high-running excitement, which but yesterday seemed to roll like an agitated sea. You are told in large capitals that if the candidates of the other ticket are elected, the commonweal needs must perish; our liberty, happiness, national honor are lost: close by, sticks another huge paper, which declares, in equally measured terms, that the opposite side is composed of a set of Catalinas at least, a nest of designing demagogues, corrupt, sold, and panting for the people's money. They tell you that orphans and widows, whose money has been squandered away, call upon you to vote against the opposite candidate; they warn you to look well at your ticket before you throw it into the ballot-box, because spurious ones have been circulated by their opponents, to whom all means are fair.

Perhaps Lieber was exaggerating, or perhaps the passing of the generations has been marked by some improvements in our conduct of elections. Yet we know that the very word "politics" often carries a moral stench. Certainly the political process is commonly marked by falsification and misrepresentation. One of the major purposes of education should be the raising of the moral, as well as the intellectual, level of the struggle for office and the shaping of policy. The corruption of this process tends to destroy faith in free institutions and to encourage resort to violence and the overthrow of popular government. To be sure, Lieber tells us that the "morning after" an election one may "walk through the quiet streets." May it ever be so! But this is not enough. Today, as we face the challenge of military dictatorships and totalitarian systems, as the eyes of the world are upon us as never before, we must strive to set an example that will encourage others to rally to the standard of political liberty and democracy.

Closely related to the issue of political integrity is that of individual responsibility for the maintenance of the foundation of our liberties, not just for today, but for tomorrow and the days after tomorrow. Many of our citizens seem to assume that this system is a gift of nature and that its essence is the right of the citizen to do whatsoever he pleases, provided he lives within the law. Carl Becker, one of our foremost students of the founding of the Republic, observed a generation ago in his *Freedom and Responsibility in the American Way of Life* that with every right or freedom goes a responsibility. Yet even in a hotly contested presidential election from a third to a half of the eligible voters fail to go to the polls and exercise rights bought with the "blood, sweat, and tears" of their ancestors. And to meet successfully the dangers and trials which clearly lie ahead we may be called upon to surpass in virtue and understanding any earlier generation. This does not mean that we should establish a system of compulsory voting or that those who now fail to exercise the franchise would raise the level of the political process by merely going to the polls. In all probability most of them and multitudes of others never take the trouble of preparing themselves to understand the issues and personalities at stake in an election. Clearly, Election Day, focus and symbol of democratic constitutional government, a government of free men under law, should ever be regarded as a veritable "holy day." But even then the total process of election should not be regarded as a ritual to be followed, but rather as a sacred responsibility to be discharged at the highest moral and intellectual level. The survival of human freedom requires from the individual citizen sacrifice and yet more sacrifice. The price of liberty, wherever it exists, comes high. And those who enjoy the blessings of liberty without paying for them are not free men but rather parasites living on the virtues and energies of others. They may even be regarded as idiots in the original Greek meaning of the term: persons who "remain aloof from communal activities" and are concerned only with "private affairs."

This leads us to another of the intangibles—devotion to the general welfare, to concern for the common good. The crucial nature of this factor was clearly expressed more than two centuries ago by Montesquieu in his *Spirit of the Laws*. In this great work the author discusses the three systems of government known to history—despotism, aristocracy, and republic. The mark of the first, he writes, is fear; of the second, honor; and of the third, virtue. And by virtue he means "love of the laws and of our country," a love which "requires a constant preference of public to private interest." And since this involves "self-renunciation" which "is ever arduous and painful," it is in a "republican government that the whole power of education is required." To inspire virtue in this sense "ought to be the principal business of education." How well we are doing in this realm is revealed in a careful study of American opinion involving all segments of the population by Samuel Stouffer entitled *Communism, Conformity and Civil Liberties,* published in 1955. He found that when asked what they "worry about most" eighty per cent of the men and women interviewed answered *solely* in terms of immediate personal and family problems. Ten per cent "professed no worries about any problems." And less than one per cent, "by the most generous interpretation," expressed any concern over the threat of Communism or the condition of civil liberties. It is not surprising that the veteran in politics commonly advises an inexperienced candidate for public office to stress the "bread and butter issues." The defense and advancement of the general welfare are further imperilled by the necessary existence in a free society of powerful organized groups, particularly in the economic sphere, which appear to be primarily concerned with the promotion of the special interests of the members. The morals and practices of all of these groups should be critically studied in our schools.

It is appropriate at this point to direct attention to an intangible that in a sense embraces all the others—an intangible that was most strikingly expressed in a brief after-dinner talk at the Author's Club in London in 1912 by a great British student of jurisprudence, Lord Moulton. In this address he divided the total range of human actions into three parts: "the domain of Positive Law, the domain of Free Choice, and between the two . . . the domain of Obedience to the Unenforcible." It is in this middle zone that conscience rules. In his opinion "the real greatness of a nation—its true civilization—is measured by the extent of this law of obedience to the 'unenforcible' far more truly than by the extent of its obedience to positive law, which might merely show a strong executive and timorous people." It should be noted that Lord Moulton made this perceptive pronouncement some years before the emergence of the totalitarian systems. To repeat the wise words of Learned Hand, liberty must lie "in the hearts of men and women." If it is not there, the cause of human freedom is doomed to perish. Thus, we must see that the vigor and essence of all the intangible supports of liberty rest squarely on the processes of education.

THE TOTALITARIAN MIND

Having examined the major intangible supports of liberty, let us turn briefly to the negative side of the issue. We must avoid, as we would avoid the plague, for that is precisely what it is to a free society—"the totalitarian mind." While elements of this mind are as old as human history, the full conception, as we know it, is of recent origin and is moulded by the forces of industrial society. It has been forged in this century by the victorious advances of Russian Communism, Italian Fascism, and German National Socialism. That the latter two were launched ostensibly to combat the first should be illuminating to the student of contemporary events in our own society. As we all know, the totalitarian scourge brought on the Second World War, and today in its Communist variant holds in bondage over one-third of the human race, penetrates every society on the planet, and is committed to the destruction of the spirit of freedom throughout the earth.

The major features of the totalitarian mind are written large in the history of this tragic epoch. Although there are differences between leaders and followers, the following characteristics would seem to give us a fairly trustworthy portrait of this type of mind, whether Communist, Fascist, or Nazi:

1. The totalitarian regards as right whatever advances his cause, or whatever he thinks will advance his cause. He completely subordinates means to ends. In the words of the notorious "Catechism of a Revolutionist" formulated in Russia in the eighteen-sixties, by Michael Bakunin or Sergei Nechaiev or by both, "to him whatever aids the triumph of the revolution is ethical; everything that hinders it is unethical and criminal."

2. He repudiates the idea of objective truth and defines as truth whatever aids his cause. His ethics are the ethics of war. One need only look for confirmation in Soviet histories and Nazi anthropologies. Moreover, in his struggle for power he will promise anything and everything calculated to arouse discontent and to attract the discontented.

3. He repudiates the idea of human dignity. He is utterly ruthless and is prepared to liquidate families,

classes, nations, or races. And he may do these things in the name of liberty, equality, and fraternity.

4. He glorifies the role of violence in both word and deed in history. He speaks incessantly of struggle, battle, and war, even as he proclaims his dedication to peace. He deliberately arouses and exploits prejudices, hatreds, and passions. He thinks in terms of castor oil, slippery elm clubs, forced labor camps, machine guns, and execution chambers.

5. He outlaws freedom of speech and thought, and even freedom of silence. He labels all criticism as treason and prohibits the formation of rival parties and organizations. He is guided by the following principle contained in a Russian revolutionary proclamation of 1862: "Remember that whoever is not with us is against us, that whoever is against us is our enemy, and that an enemy must be exterminated by all possible means."

6. He seeks to control all agencies and processes for the molding and informing of the minds of both young and old. In this effort he overlooks nothing from the school and the theatre to the calendar and the circus. His motto is: "Control everything."

7. He performs all of his acts in the name of his class, his people, his nation, or his race—in the name of patriotism, public safety, or love of "all progressive mankind." And he does this without consulting those in whose name he speaks.

8. He is certain of the rightness of his policies and the grandeur of his mission in history, whether he appeals to the authority of "blood" or the "laws of social development," which he alone understands.

9. He rejects completely the conception of the higher law—the law above the state. He rejects the right of conscience, for he is God.

This totalitarian mind has penetrated our society. It is found, of course, in its purest form perhaps in the Communist Party. But, as an expression of the dialectical process in history, it is found also in some individuals and organizations which would combat the Communist menace by appropriating its morals and methods and by thus destroying our own most precious freedoms. The study of totalitarianism and the totalitarian mind should constitute an essential element in education for human freedom.

THE AMERICAN WAY OF LIFE

It would seem fitting to close this lecture with a few words about "The American Way of Life." Here is an expression that is commonly employed to condemn in the name of patriotism any proposal to change our institutions. Yet our record since the founding of the Republic is marked generation after generation by profound changes—changes utterly unanticipated by the men who assembled in the Constitutional Convention in 1787. At the turn of the eighteenth century the proposal to abolish all laws of primogeniture and entail, survivals from the age of feudalism, precipitated a most bitter struggle. The liberation of the Negro slaves was achieved only by a prolonged and bloody civil war. And even today, a century after the Emancipation Proclamation, white supremacy is regarded in many parts of the nation as an essential ingredient of the American Way of Life and as a great bulwark against the spread of Communism. At one time Protestant supremacy or Anglo-Saxon supremacy was similarly regarded by many. The same may be said of the patriarchal family and the denial of political rights to women. Consider also the passing of the self-contained rural household and the early agrarian society in the "age of homespun." Here indeed was a cataclysmic transformation of the ancient and revered American Way of Life. In the Constitutional Convention Gouverneur Morris estimated that nine-tenths of the people were freeholders, ignoring of course the Negro slaves. Jefferson based his political faith on the continuing of this condition. "Those who labor in the earth," he wrote in 1782, "are the chosen people of God, if ever he had a chosen people, whose breasts he has made his peculiar deposit for substantial and genuine virtue.... The mobs of great cities add just so much to the support of pure government, as sores do to the strength of the human body." It would appear that the essentials of the American Way of Life have long since passed away.

Some of the great inventions of the first half of the nineteenth century, including the railroad, the telegraph, and even the Erie Canal, were vigorously opposed by many stalwart citizens. The same may be said of advances in medicine, such as vaccination against smallpox, and anaesthesia to relieve the pains of childbirth. And the battle in the Congress over the income tax in the eighteen-nineties was extremely bitter. To the opponents of the measure this was an attack on the sacred institution of private property and consequently on the very essence of the American Way of Life. It would seem that a substantial minority continue to feel this way about the mat-

ter. And the many changes in the role of
government in the economy have been
and are greeted today in the same man-
ner. We still employ such expressions as
"economic individualism," the "free en-
terprise system," and "government in-
tervention in business" in the spirit of
the nineteenth century—the century to
which many Americans ostensibly would
like to return. The development of science and technology, of course, has de-
creed otherwise. I personally would have
preferred to live in the time of Daniel
Boone, but learned early in life that this
was not possible!

All of this leads to the question: Does
the expression, "The American Way of
Life" have any meaning whatsoever?
Does it mean anything more or less than
the total complex of the behavior patterns, the institutional forms, the body
of ideals and values, and the life conditions of our people at any given time?
The answer is a vigorous and unqualified
affirmative. But to find the answer we
shall have to probe more deeply into the
history of our people and our institu-

tions. In fact, it is to be found in our Constitution and Bill of Rights, in our tradition of political liberty and popular rule. It is stated clearly in the third edition of the first textbook in American history used in our schools. The book was published in 1807 and the author was a Philadelphia printer, John McCulloch. In reporting the election of 1800 the author writes: "And it is the glory of our republican government that the people have the supreme controul; and that when they apprehend that their rulers err, they can effect a change of measures at the periods of election without tumult, or the hazard of revolution." Clearly, if the expression has any meaning, here it is. More than a century later, George Herbert Meade, one of our great philosophers, confirmed the judgment of John McCulloch. Our political system, he said, is a system for the "institutionalization of revolution." The essence of the American Way of Life thus rests on the boldest and most generous conception of the nature of man known to the history of politics and government. Today in this vast, complex, and dynamic world, marked by unprecedented challenges and the perpetual emergence of the unexpected, our way of life is being and will be tested as never before. To prepare for this test of popular liberty should be the active purpose of American education, lest "that government of the people, by the people, for the people ... perish from the earth."